Mind Your Manners
At Parties

Arianna Candell / Rosa M. Curto

BARRON'S

Parties are a lot of fun!

Wow! Quite a few children are attending Mark's party. Parties are so much fun! When we're invited to somebody's house and there are lots of other kids there, we have to be careful with their belongings. If we all behave, we can enjoy ourselves thoroughly.

Inviting people

Today is Mark's birthday, and he has invited his friends over. He asked all of his classmates to attend, because he doesn't want any of them to feel left out.

Mark is a little nervous since it's almost time for the party, and he would like everything to go really well.

Getting ready

Laura has very long hair, but she doesn't like to have it brushed or braided. Since she is going to Mark's party, she has promised her friend Lee to have her hair brushed and braided to look pretty.

So many presents!

Mark has received many presents including storybooks and toys. Julia even made him a very colorful friendship bracelet. Helen was so eager for Mark to open her present that she tore off the wrapping paper as she was giving it to him! Now she realizes that her friend would have had a better surprise if she had let him open the gift.

Party time!

After Mark opens the presents, the children play and have a great time. When it is time to eat, they all sit down and put their napkins on their laps. Adrian kneels on his chair and says he wants to look taller and be able to reach farther.

Annie, who is sitting next to him, tells him to sit down properly so he won't make a mess by dropping things on the floor. Adrian listens to Annie and sits down.

Use good table manners

Peter stuffs his mouth with food, talks with his mouth full, and makes bubbles with his drinking straw. He is so hungry that he picks up food with his fingers. Then he wipes them on his T-shirt! When Jamie sees this, he tells Peter that his behavior is not nice for others to watch. Peter then unfolds his napkin, wipes his face, and uses his fork.

What a delicious-looking cake! While Mark thinks of a wish, John seems eager to blow out the candles. Julia has to remind John that it's not his birthday! When it's your birthday, it will be your turn to think of a wish and blow out the candles.

Who is blowing out the candles?

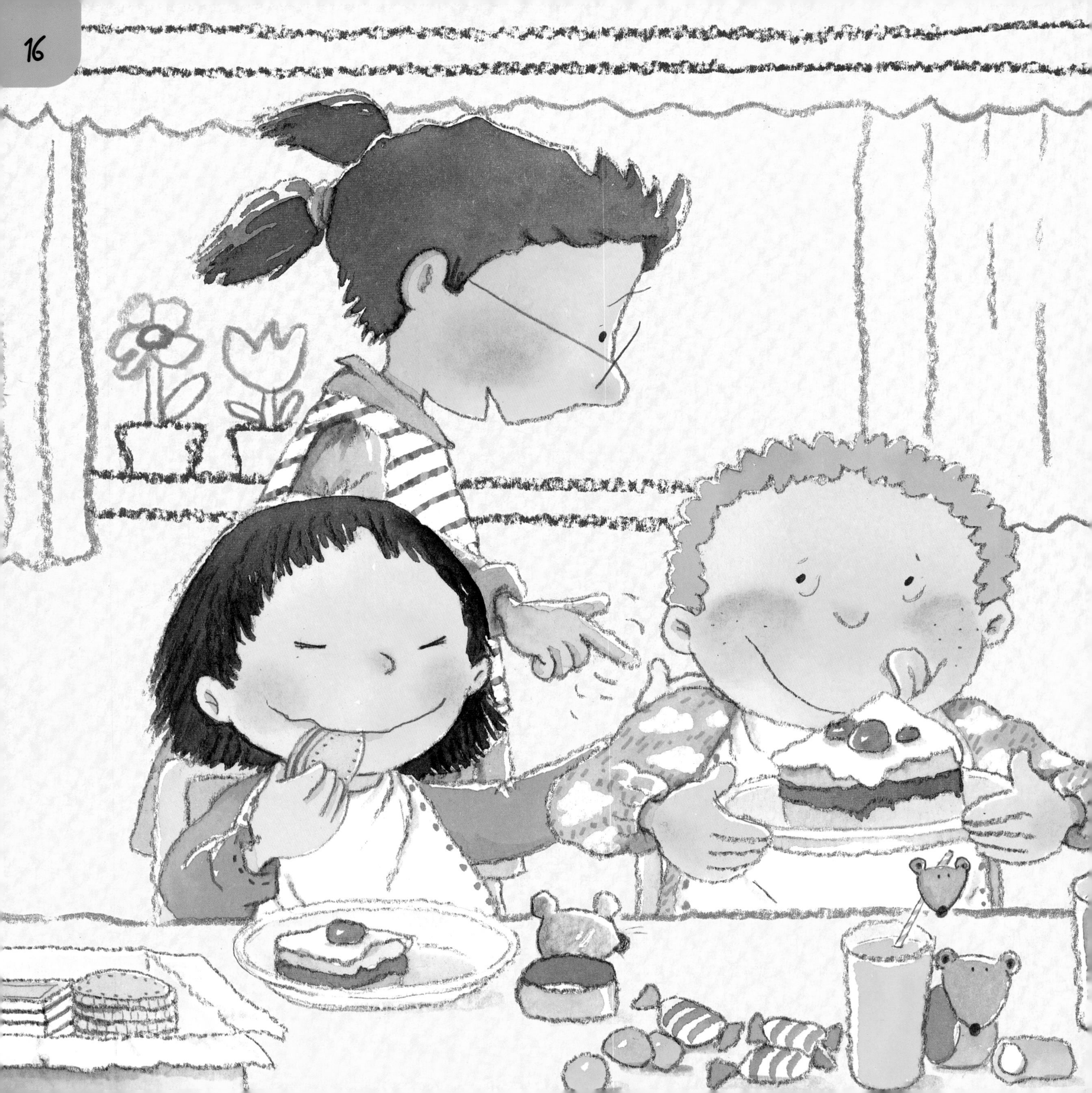

May I have some more?

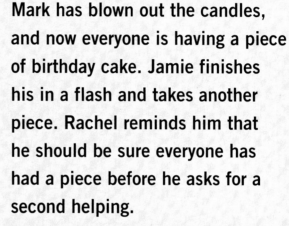

Mark has blown out the candles, and now everyone is having a piece of birthday cake. Jamie finishes his in a flash and takes another piece. Rachel reminds him that he should be sure everyone has had a piece before he asks for a second helping.

Jamie does ask if everyone has had a piece of cake. Since all of the other kids have a full plate, he asks politely for a second piece.

No shouting, please

Mark's grandparents, uncles, and aunts have also come to his birthday party. They are grownups and feel uncomfortable when the children all talk loudly at the same time. When Rachel and Mary play together, they like to shout but don't realize it. When Paul hears them, he reminds them that they can still play without shouting as if they're at the playground. Mary and Rachel play more quietly so that everyone can have a good time.

No running inside

Paul and Mark run up and down the hallway chasing each other. Suddenly, they knock over a vase and some books from an end table. Nothing breaks, but the kids get a good scare! Now they remember that they should not run inside the house. They can chase one another when they play in the park.

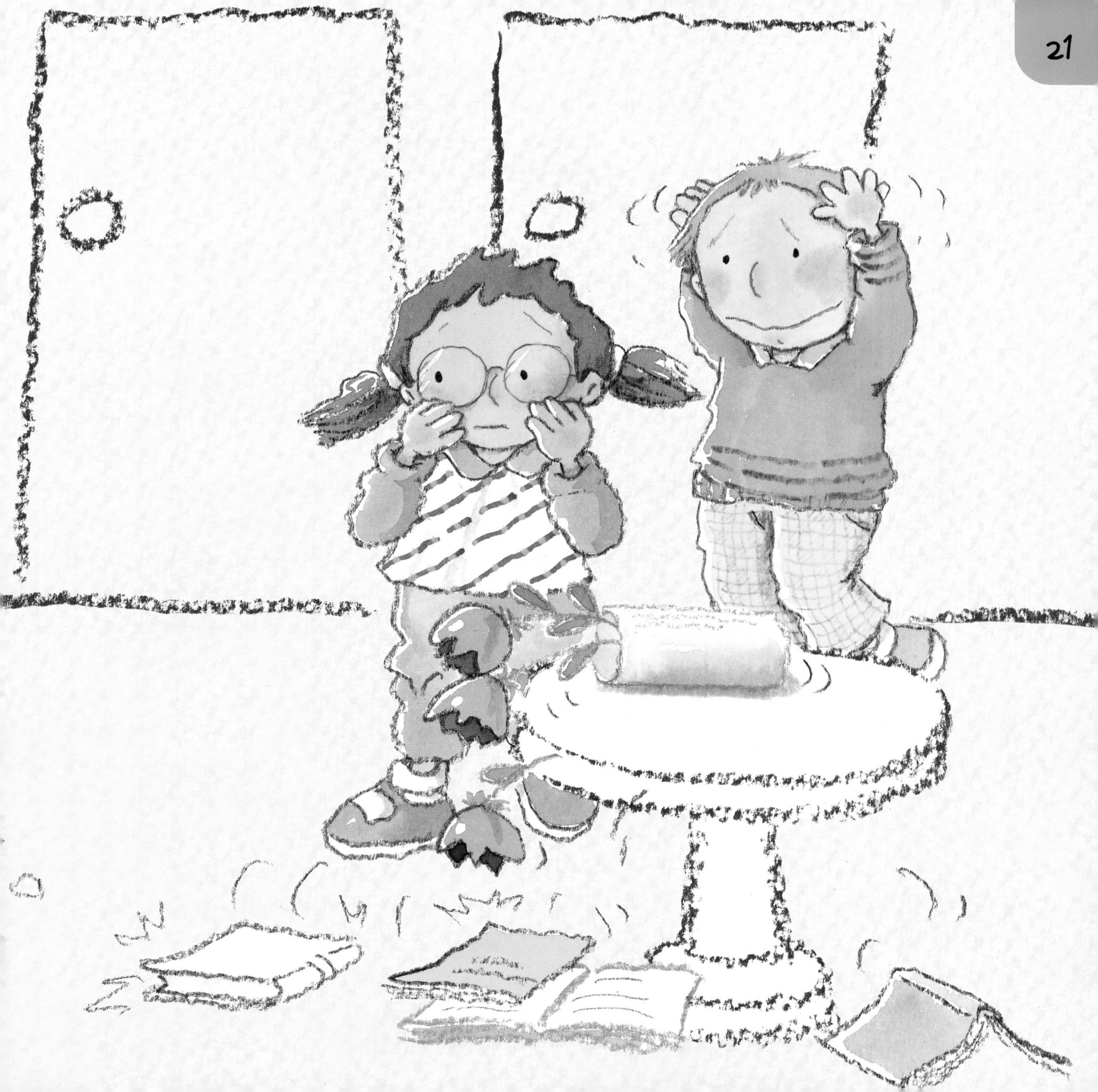

Cleaning up

It's almost time to go home, and soon the parents will be coming to get their children. Everything is quite messy since the kids have been playing so much. Paul knows that they all should help to clean up so one person will not have to do it all. All of the children help, and soon everything is back in order.

Camera ready

Mark wants to have a photo taken of
his birthday party with all his friends.
Helen doesn't like to have her picture
taken, so instead of smiling, she
frowns! Mark tells her that she'll
be sorry when she sees the photo
later. For the next photo, Helen
makes a big smile!

Thank you and good bye

The party is over, and it's time for the children to leave. When Julie's parents come to get her, she says she doesn't want to leave. She wants to stay a little longer because she is having such a good time.

Helen tells her it is time to leave now, and they will come back another time. Julie realizes that her friend is right. She says good bye and thanks Mark and his parents for inviting her to such a wonderful party.

What a party!

The party is finally over. Everyone has gone home, and Mark has time to remember all the fun. The children had such a good time, and it has been an unforgettable day!

Activities

BALLOONS

It's nice to have balloons at your party. Get a variety of colorful balloons, and ask a grownup to help you blow them up. Once blown up, use broad-tipped markers to make nice drawings on them. Your friends will say they are the best looking balloons they've ever seen!

A PARTY HOST

Keep several things in mind when you are organizing a birthday party. Parents usually prepare all the activities, but children can cooperate in many ways and can help by offering some good ideas.

HOT CHOCOLATE

When we invite friends to our house, we like to offer them something to eat and drink. Almost everyone enjoys a good cup of hot cocoa or chocolate. It's easy to make, but ask a grownup to help you. Here are the steps to follow: Get all of the ingredients: milk, powdered cocoa and sugar, or just chocolate syrup. Begin by pouring some milk in a pan (the quantity will depend on the number of people). Ask a grownup to heat the mixture. When the milk starts to boil, add the cocoa and some sugar or add just chocolate syrup. Stir the mix constantly. When it is all mixed, it will be ready to serve and share with your friends.

A CUP FOR EACH GUEST

When there are several people at a party, it's hard for them to keep track of their cup. To avoid this, make a picture on each plastic or paper cup representing the face of each guest. If you are able to, you can write their names under the drawings.

SAYING THANK YOU

How can you say a special thank you to your guests who have brought you presents? Here is an idea:

Make picture frames out of construction paper or cardboard. Inside of each frame, tape a photo of your friends at the party. Then add a little thank-you note and mention the gift that was given to you. Ask for help from a grownup if needed. Your friends will have a very nice surprise!

Guidelines for parents

GETTING READY

Getting ready to go to a party is an important part of the exciting day. Explain to the children that it's important to look our best when we have been invited to a party or when we are meeting someone new to us. When we give a party, it's fun to see everyone looking their best. When it's our turn to attend someone else's party, we should also look our best for them and for ourselves.

WHEN CHILDREN PLAY TOGETHER

Children often get very excited when they are with other children, and it may be difficult for them to behave. Parties and get-togethers are usually noisy, but we can explain to the children that they can still have fun without shouting, running, or disturbing the guest's property. When they have some guidelines, they can play without constant adult reminders to behave.

HELPFUL REMINDERS

Getting children ready to go out may seem to be an overwhelming task. In general, parents are often concerned about how their children will behave on special occasions or functions.

To have a peaceful day (or at least as peaceful as possible), we may use many ideas presented in this text. These suggestions about party behavior can be extended to those occasions when we go out with our own children...to a restaurant, to visit grandparents, to a friend's house, family parties, and so forth. With a little initial explanation about good behavior, going out with our children can be an enjoyable experience. In your explanation, include what you will do, where you will go, who you will see, and so forth. Anticipate the misbehavior that may occur, and let your children know what behaviors they should avoid and why!

EATING MANNERS

Children may have been taught good table manners, but they often don't use them when they are with other people. They may misbehave or act silly. Before the event, remind them that they should use forks to eat and napkins to wipe their face. They should not talk with their mouths full, and they need to avoid silly behavior such as blowing bubbles through their drinking straws! It is also important to remind them not to get up from the table until they are excused. They should also ask politely before having a second helping.

Also remind them that good table manners should be observed at home as well as when they are at a party or a restaurant.

First English language edition for the United States and Canada published in 2005 by
Barron's Educational Series, Inc.

Original title of the book in Catalan: *Com ens hem de comportar a les festes*
© 2005 Gemser Publications, S.L.
Author: Arianna Candell
Illustrator: Rosa M. Curto

All inquiries should be addressed to:
Barron's Educational Series, Inc.
250 Wireless Boulevard
Hauppauge, New York 11788
www.barronseduc.com

International Standard Book No. 0-7641-3167-2
Library of Congress Catalog Card No. 2004111320

Printed in Spain
9 8 7 6 5 4 3 2 1